THE LITTLE BOOK OF DIANA

Written by Ian and Claire Welch

THE LITTLE BOOK OF DIANA

This edition first published in the UK in 2007
by Green Umbrella Publishing

© Green Umbrella Publishing 2007

www.greenumbrella.co.uk

Publishers Jules Gammond, Vanessa Gardner

Printed and bound in China

ISBN 978-1-906229-25-2

Contents

Introduction

PERHAPS NEVER BEFORE, AND never again, has one life touched the hearts of so many, been the subject of much gossip and speculation – even in death – and been so loved, adored and cherished by a nation. Yet, this is exactly what the late Diana, Princess of Wales, achieved in her extraordinary, short-lived life. It has been 10 years (31 August 1997) since that fateful night when the Princess, trying to escape the glare of the cameras, climbed into a car from the back entrance to the Ritz Hotel in Paris. The car, chased by the paparazzi, crashed and the death of the Princess shook the world.

Even before Lady Diana Spencer married the Prince of Wales in 1981 the whole nation was infatuated with her. Who was she? What was she like? What was she wearing? And, what did she

have to say? From the moment that the press knew that the Prince might have a serious relationship that could see the heir to the throne marry in his thirties, Diana was surrounded by intrigue and newspaper articles with everyone wanting to know everything there possibly was to know about her. It was as if she became royal and public property all at the same time and there was little help to guide this young, shy and sensitive woman into the new high-profile life that awaited her.

As a young woman, Diana was blossoming and beautiful. But, the formal life into which she had been born and the restricted lifestyle to which she was accustomed were about to cocoon her. When her marriage was finally over and the restrictions gone Diana came into her own. Her beauty

grew, her self-esteem flourished and her charitable work was quite simply outstanding, compelling and moving. Her gift for relating to everyone made her an instant hit with all whom she met and, despite those who were critical of her, Diana was an incredible woman and mother whose unconditional love reached millions. Even certain First Ladies and Hollywood legends fade in significance against the iconic Diana, Princess of Wales.

Chapter 1

Althorp and the Spencer family

THE ESTATE OF ALTHORP BEGAN its journey into the history books in 1508 and has been the ancestral home of the Spencer family since that time. It covers 14,000 acres which include villages, woodlands, farmland and cottages across the Northamptonshire, Warwickshire and Norfolk landscape. The estate is managed from Althorp itself by an experienced team who work in farming, property management, events and marketing, gamekeeping, gardening, housekeeping, forestry and other areas. The aim of the estate today is to carry out good land management practices which include conservation and maintaining the rural environment while combining this with commercial based activities all of which contribute to the local economy.

RIGHT The first Earl, John Spencer

EARL SPENCER

ABOVE The main staircase at Althorp in 1822

But, it all began in farming in 1486, with John Spencer, who was tenant at Althorp, and his nephew John, through livestock trading. The Spencer family were sheep farmers and nephew, John Spencer, eventually bought both Althorp and Wormleighton Hall, setting the scene for a family that were to come to prominence historically and politically, and who were destined to become an important part of British nobility. In later generations, marriage

ABOVE Countess Lavinia Spencer, wife of the 2nd Earl, George John Spencer, the statesman and famous collector of books

the richest men in the United Kingdom and travelled to court with James I in 1603. The Spencer family, when Lord Spencer was ennobled, like many other noble families, then found themselves in public service. The family flourished and with foresight, intellect and hard work became one of the most established and high-profile families in the country. Robert's son William – the second Lord Spencer – built a racecourse at Althorp, while his own son, Henry, an Oxford graduate, fought in the Civil War where he was fatally wounded. Henry's marriage to the daughter of the Earl of Southampton resulted in his own son Robert, who was a notorious politician, becoming the second Earl of Sunderland.

Family members came and went and by the early 1700s the 5th Earl also became the 3rd Duke of Marlborough, but in 1734, the Earl left Althorp and the Sunderland title was lost. The Earl's brother, John Spencer, inherited Althorp as well as much wealth and fortune from other family members but died soon after leaving the family fortune to his 12-year-old son, also named John. As he grew up, this astute young man used his wealth to commis-

led the family into the peerage while sound business practices amassed a fortune and Robert Spencer (1570–1627) became the first Lord Spencer. With an income of around £8,000 per annum, Lord Spencer became one of

ALTHORP AND THE SPENCER FAMILY

sion the artist Reynolds for portraits of his family – today these are much revered and valued – and he became one of the leading patrons of the arts. In 1761, he became Baron and Viscount Spencer and took the title Earl Spencer – the first – four years later. Women in the Spencer family were undoubtedly strong and forthright and the 2nd Earl seems to have been overshadowed by both his wife, Lavinia, and his sister, Georgiana, Duchess of Devonshire. But, the 2nd Earl did make his own great contribution to Althorp when he amassed the greatest private library anywhere in the world which included more than 40,000 manuscripts. As well as having an obsession with books, the Earl also had a renowned political life and became First Lord of the Admiralty under Pitt (1794–1826). The Earl's son, John Charles, Viscount Althorp, also entered Parliament but joined with radicals to create social reform. He dedicated himself to politics on the death of his wife and rose to Chancellor of the Exchequer and he was instrumental in the Reform Bill.

Throughout the history of the Spencer family, field sports and politics went hand in hand and the 5th Earl,

John Poyntz was no exception. He was – like some of his fore-bearers – driven by duty rather than ambition and became known as the Red Earl on account of his

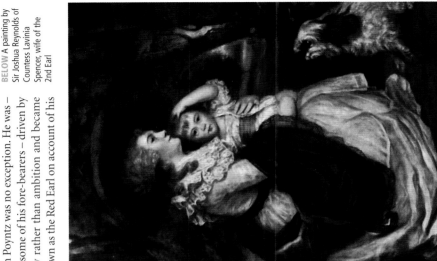

BELOW A painting by Sir Joshua Reynolds of Countess Lavinia Spencer, wife of the 2nd Earl

ALTHORP AND THE SPENCER FAMILY

RIGHT John Poyntz the 5th Earl Spencer, known as The Red Earl owing to his distinctive red beard

BELOW John Charles Spencer, 3rd Earl, Lord Althorp, statesman and sportsman. He led the fight for the passing of the Reform Bill of 1832

red beard. Having been at the centre of a great deal of activity for generations, Althorp was to receive some care and attention when Jack Spencer the 7th Earl took the title while his wife, Countess Spencer, was renowned for her visits to the sick and infirm. His son, Johnnie, formerly Viscount Althorp and 8th Earl and his wife, Frances Roche, had five children: Sarah (born in 1956), Jane (1957), John (1960), Diana (1961) and Charles (1964).

Charles, the 9th Earl, currently combines Althorp as a family home and a commercially successful estate which welcomes thousands of visitors world-wide each year. Between July and

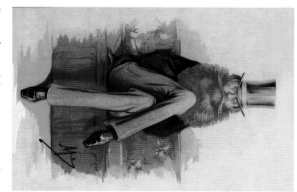

September, visitors are invited to explore the house and park at Althorp with its magnificent Round Oval. There is also a renowned exhibition "Diana: A Celebration" which covers the life and work of the late Princess of Wales. As Althorp has been a family home for more than 500 years visitors can experience for themselves the welcoming atmosphere of this somewhat austere looking house and marvel at the

ALTHORP AND THE SPENCER FAMILY

paintings, furniture, sculptures and china that have been collected over many generations by this high-profile family. Althorp also hosts a number of events during each season it is open to the public and there is a literary festival, summer Shakespeare as well as charitable events including the Macmillan Cancer Support Walk. Set in the estate, Althorp is walled within 550 acres of parkland and today offers corporate hospitality that is tailored to the individual event's requirements while the shop houses a wide variety of gifts all of which have been approved by the Spencer family.

THE LITTLE BOOK OF DIANA | 11

Chapter 2

Early Life

DESPITE APPEARANCES AND A privileged background with grand estates and noble ancestors, the Honourable Diana Spencer was born into a difficult life on 1 July 1961. The third daughter for Earl Spencer and his wife Frances, Diana was not the longed-for heir, however, she was loved and adored by her parents. Sadly though, the death of her brother John one year before her own birth may have been the catalyst that began the downward spiral that her parents' marriage was to experience. After two daughters – Sarah and Jane – John was heir to the Spencer estate. However, he lived only a few short hours. Not only were Diana's parents grieving for their son, but family members thought that Frances should undergo tests to see why she was unable to produce a healthy son and

heir. The experience for the future mother of four – including a healthy son to take the Earldom – was humiliating and pointless. Of course, we now know that the sex of a baby is determined by the father, but in 1960, medical knowledge was limited and the then current thinking was the opposite.

The family lived at Park House when Diana Frances Spencer was born – although the infant was not named for a week – as her parents had so anticipated that she would be a boy they had not considered any names for a girl. Even though the Spencers loved their youngest daughter they were disappointed that an heir had not yet been born to the family. Diana was christened in Sandringham church, yet when her brother Charles was born some three years later, he was christened at

LEFT Viscount Althorp, son of the Earl and Countess Spencer with his fiancée, 18-year-old Hon Frances Roche, daughter of Lord and Lady Fermoy, 1955

RIGHT Diana on her first birthday at Park House, Sandringham

Westminster Abbey with the Queen as one of his godparents.

Park House, in Norfolk, was Diana's first home. The house was acquired by her mother's family, the Fermoys, when Maurice Fermoy, the 4th Baron was granted the lease of Park House by George V. The building had originally been constructed to accommodate guests and staff from nearby Sandringham. Maurice Fermoy – Diana's grandfather – was the Conservative MP for King's Lynn, while his wife founded the King's Lynn Festival for Arts and Music. Park House was where the young Diana felt safe and at home. Visiting Althorp to see her grandparents was not something she relished. Her ability to relate to people on all levels from all walks of life with or without illness – whether physical or mental – was outstanding and was probably in part inherited from her paternal grandmother, Countess Spencer, whom she loved dearly. However, she was somewhat wary of her grandfather with whom her own father had a tenuous relationship. Compared to the austere Althorp, Park House was

RIGHT Diana playing with her brother Charles in the grounds of Park House when she was six years old

small and comfortable and Diana loved her cat Marmalade – a bad-tempered animal that wasn't as popular with other members of her family – and their spaniel Jill. Diana was a keen horse rider in her younger years and like her sisters before her was in the saddle at an early age. She developed an incredible passion for animals, although it seems as if the smaller the animal the better. Diana and younger brother Charles were also known to visit the grave of their brother John in Sandringham churchyard which may have led to Diana having feelings of guilt for not being the longed-for boy.

When Diana was ready to be tutored downstairs in the family home her sisters Sarah and Jane were at West Heath School in Kent as boarders. With a nanny and staff, the young Diana did not see as much of her parents as she needed, or would have liked to. Her childhood very much resembled that of a bygone era – in much the same way her own parents' did – in that mealtimes were spent with the nanny in the nursery and parents were a distant presence. This would have been difficult for an already "guilty" Diana who craved the love of her parents. Materially, she and

her siblings lacked for nothing, but emotionally they were all left to their own devices. Today, it is known and widely written that children thrive on emotional support from their parents. It was a little-known of or cared about issue in the 1960s.

The marriage between the Earl and Countess Spencer was failing and failing fast and the children left at home – Diana and Charles – were party to some heated arguments. Diana was just six years old when her mother and father decided to separate and she watched as her mother got in a car and drove down the drive and out of her daily life. Both children were deeply affected by their parents' separation and subsequent divorce. The divorce itself was acrimonious and difficult – as is often the case – and although it is usual for the mother to be granted custody of the children, in this particular case, the Earl was given custody as is more common when the father is a nobleman. With more clout and more money behind him, the Earl was assured of victory over his former wife. However, most warring parents want to be the stable influence in their children's lives and the Earl and Frances Spencer were no

RIGHT Diana as an
eight-year-old

different. But, sometimes children don't just "bounce back" and although they may accept the new situation they find themselves in, it does not mean that they are thriving on it.

Diana was compassionate and sensitive and felt her parents' divorce very deeply. It seems that there was no-one to whom she could really turn and both she and Charles appear to have put grit and determination into their acceptance of the situation – and ultimately – their survival. It was unusual for couples to divorce when the Spencers finally accepted the breakdown in their relationship and decided to call things a day. For children there was no understanding or ways of helping them through the difficult times that lay ahead. Their father was sad and was prone to periods of silence while their mother would cry. Over the past 20 years or so much has been written and documented about the effects of divorce on children and today there is a great deal of understanding and help available. For the Spencer children there was nothing of the kind.

When the 7th Earl, Jack Spencer died in 1975, the family left their former home and moved to Althorp. But, Park House always remained special to Diana and she would visit even when her former home became a hotel for the disabled. By now, Frances was living in London and had begun a relationship with Peter Shand Kydd. When Peter and Frances married in May 1969, Diana and Charles found a stepfather who was relaxed and demonstrative with the children. They liked him immediately and he took them sailing from his and their mother's home on the West Sussex coast. Diana remained loyal to her father, while building her relationship with her new stepfather, even though the Earl found it difficult to relate to his children and was not particularly relaxed around them. It seems as if father and children loved each other dearly, but none found the words to make things easier. In 1972, the Shand Kydds moved to the Isle of Seil in Argyllshire where summer holidays were idyllic and fun for the young children. Childhood provided Diana with the opportunity to excel at swimming and dancing, although having broken an arm while riding, she became anxious about it and never matured into a confident horsewoman.

Riddlesworth Hall, near Park House,

RIGHT 14-year-old Diana being kissed by her pet pony 'Soufflé'

was the school that Diana attended where her swimming and dancing were allowed and encouraged to develop. She was just nine years old when she first arrived and at first was confused and resented her situation. Despite the fact that the Earl found it difficult to communicate with his children, Diana felt the loss of him badly by starting at boarding school. However, there were plus sides and Diana was allowed to keep her guinea pig, Peanuts, with her. At Riddlesworth Hall, Diana found her own niche and was actually quite happy. She was a popular pupil and found that other girls, like herself, came from "broken homes". Despite her friends and her popularity, Diana herself claimed that she knew she was separate and that life would take her in a different direction. She remained, as she had been in her earlier life, a loner. What did worry Diana were her academic abilities. Both her older sisters were fairly academic and Charles eventually went to Oxford University. Diana followed her sisters to West Heath, but failed all her 'O' levels with D grades. However, she excelled in ways in which the rest of her family did not.

One of these special ways which

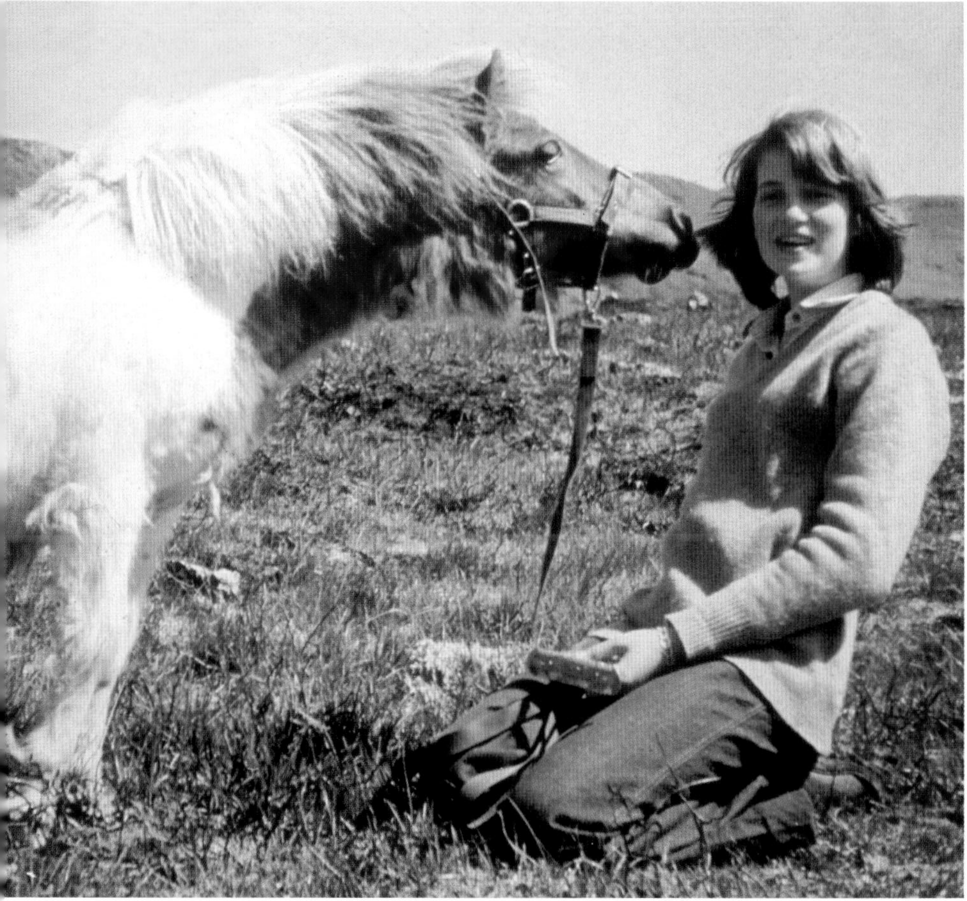

showed the young Diana's true charac-
ter was by visiting the old, sick and
infirm (something her paternal grandmother had also done near Althorp)
which was encouraged by her school.
She also took part in the Voluntary
Service Unit which saw her visit
Darenth Park near Dartford. The hospital was home to mentally and physically
disabled people along with severely
disturbed teenagers. Although it was
encouraged, perhaps it was also instinc-
tive that Diana would get down on her
hands and knees to interact with the
hospital's patients. Diana's natural
aptitude shone through and her
achievements with those she met helped
to build her self-esteem.

When her father became Earl Spencer
in 1975, Diana became Lady Diana
Spencer. Her sisters also became Ladies
and Charles became Viscount Althorp.
Diana was respectful of her older sister
Jane, who compared to Sarah seemed
to be sensible. However, she hero-
worshipped Sarah and would wait at
Althorp for her older sibling to arrive
from London. Parties at the house were
exciting but it seems none of the family
was prepared for the arrival of the
daughter of Barbara Cartland, Raine,

FAR LEFT Diana in the Western Isles of Scotland, 1974

LEFT Diana during a summer holiday in Itchenor, West Sussex

RIGHT Raine who was allegedly referred to by Diana and her siblings as Acid Raine

London Council (GLC). The determined, tough, challenging lady first came into the Earl's children's lives in the early 1970s. Although Jack Spencer was taken with Raine, his grandchildren were less so. The couple married quietly in 1977 and the children were unaware of the event. Relations between Raine and the Earl's four children were set for battle for some time to come. Diana kept her cool with her stepmother for more than 10 years, then finally she exploded at a rehearsal for Charles's wedding to Victoria Lockwood. Seated alongside Mrs Shand Kydd, Raine Spencer refused to talk to her stepchildren's mother. Diana rounded on her step-mother in anger. Later, Frances Shand Kydd is reported to have said that it

was the first time that anyone in her family had stood up for her – even her own mother had sided with the Earl in their 1968 divorce proceedings.

Earl Spencer and the former Lady Lewisham and Countess of Dartmouth worked together on *What Is Our Heritage?* a book for the former Greater

Life with Raine Spencer in charge at Althorp was difficult and even Christmas has been noted in many commentaries as being arduous for the children. But, life was about to get better for the young Diana. After leaving West Heath and a spell at the Institut Alpin Videmanette finishing school in Switzerland, Diana was ready to start a new life in London.

BELOW Earl and Countess Spencer in 1981

Chapter 3

Career

DIANA DIDN'T REACH LONDON and take up a high-profile or heady career. In fact, she worked as a charlady for her sister Sarah for £1.00 an hour. With no formal qualifications – certainly no 'O' levels – and no vocational skills, Diana was unsure of what to do with her life. She had some interest in working with children and seemed destined for unskilled, low-paid jobs. However, it was traditional for aristocratic girls to marry once they finished their formal education and it was probably thought that Diana would follow suit. The Spencers certainly did not entertain the fact that Diana should have a formal career, however, they were reluctant to let her live alone in London.

In 1978, the family were in turmoil when Earl Spencer suffered a cerebral haemorrhage. He was initially cared for at Northampton General Hospital before his wife Raine had him moved to the National Hospital of Nervous Diseases in London where he lay in a coma for several months. Even the Earl's illness and bleak prognosis did little to help the family pull together and step-mother and stepchildren remained divided. Raine tried to stop the children visiting and what could have been a turning point for all concerned turned into yet more battles. Eventually, the Earl was discharged from hospital in January 1979 while Diana was undergoing a cookery course run by Elizabeth Russell in Wimbledon. Following the course, Mrs Shand Kydd asked Betty Vacani – the renowned dance teacher – to interview Diana for a job. Having been successful at the interview Diana became a student ballet teacher at the dance studio. Her time at the studio was to prove short-lived as an accident that tore her ankle tendons on the ski slopes put paid to her budding career.

In July 1979 when Diana turned 18, her parents bought her a flat at 60 Coleherne Court in London and she rented rooms to friends Carolyn Bartholomew, Sophie Kimball and Philippa Coaker. A month later, Diana was joined by new tenants Anne Bolton and Virginia Pitman, while stalwart friend, Carolyn remained a tenant. Around this time, Diana also began to branch out in her career and took a job working at the Young England Kindergarten some afternoons a week. Here, the teenager excelled, and her bosses asked her to work mornings as well. Diana also worked at this time as a private nanny to a little boy.

LEFT Lady Diana Spencer worked as a nanny and kindergarten teacher in London

Chapter 4

Wedding Fever

DIANA'S FIRST MEETING WITH THE Prince of Wales seems to have been a rather subdued affair with no "love at first sight" on a plough field on the Althorp estate. The Prince, who was at the time enjoying a romance with Diana's sister Sarah, was more intent on the day's shooting than meeting the sister of his latest love. Sarah was renowned for her competitiveness and when the Prince asked the 16-year-old Diana to show him the family picture gallery, after a dinner held in the Prince's honour, Sarah took over and Diana politely made her excuses and left them to it.

Despite a cooling in relations between Prince Charles and Lady Sarah, both she and Diana were invited to the Prince's 30th birthday party at Buckingham Palace in November 1978.

But, Prince Charles, driven by duty, had been searching for his ideal bride for some time before his relationship with Lady Sarah Spencer. It all started with the heir apparent had developed the intense scrutiny over his love life, and skill of appearing devoted to finding the country's future queen. Aged 19, the young prince first found love with Lucia Santa Cruz, the beautiful daughter of the former Chilean ambassador. Despite the couple's insistence that there was no romance, Santa Cruz was the first royal girlfriend to make it to Balmoral. However, Lucia Santa Cruz's religion presented a problem. As a Roman Catholic, marriage was deemed impossible and – as an unsuitable match – Santa Cruz's relationship with the Prince became one of friendship. It was Santa Cruz, who returned to Chile

LEFT Charles, Prince of Wales and Camilla after a polo match

WEDDING FEVER

in 1973, who introduced the Prince to a certain Camilla Shand. The vivacious 24-year-old Shand was to become his wife 33 years later.

The Prince missed out on a relationship at the time with Camilla Shand when the young woman was swept off her feet by a dashing polo player, Andrew Parker Bowles, a former equerry to the Queen. Prince Charles was away serving at sea while Parker Bowles was a former boyfriend of his sister, Princess Anne. There were other hopefuls however in the form of Lady Jane Wellesley the daughter of the 8th Duke of Wellington. Wellesley was a popular choice with the British public and the Prince dated her for 18 months. There was huge speculation that Wellesley would be a royal bride but Lady Jane didn't want the title of Princess of Wales or the lifestyle that went with it.

His relationship with Davina Sheffield looked promising until it transpired that the young beauty had lived with a lover. Sheffield, the wealthy grand-daughter of Lord McGowan, the ICI tycoon, was quickly dumped by the Prince despite the fact she had won his heart. The Prince then went on to

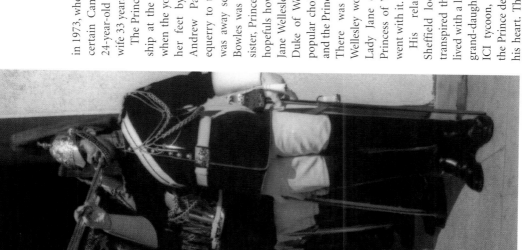

LEFT The wedding of Andrew Parker-Bowles and Camilla Shand at the Guard's Chapel, London, July 1973

have a five-year on-off relationship with Amanda Knatchbull, the grand-daughter of the late Lord Mountbatten. Despite reports of marriage proposals, Knatchbull refused the Prince and decided to further her studies at a university in China. It was in 1978 that the Prince first dated Lady Sarah Spencer. Unlike other girlfriends there was little spark between Prince Charles and Lady Sarah and he went on to date Sabrina Guinness for nine months. The last serious relationship the Prince enjoyed before becoming linked with Lady Diana was with Anna Wallace, the daughter of a wealthy Scottish landowner. Known for her fiery temper and nicknamed "Whiplash" Wallace, the relationship turned sour when Anna stormed out of the Queen Mother's birthday celebrations.

So a string of relationships had left the Prince empty-handed with no Princess of Wales yet in the offing. Lady Diana was said to have enjoyed the Prince's 30th birthday party enormously but would have been bemused if she had known that the Prince may have been considering a romance between them.

Meanwhile, Lady Diana had plenty of

boyfriends of her own, although none became her lover. They included Rory Scott, a lieutenant in the Royal Scots Guards and Adam Russell, an Oxford graduate whose decision to spend a year travelling probably cost him his relationship with Diana. Meanwhile, Diana was invited to attend a shooting weekend at Sandringham. This was some six months after Lord Mountbatten had been murdered by the IRA and the Prince's relationship with Amanda Knatchbull seemed to become closer as the two united in their grief.

In July 1980 Diana was invited to spend the weekend at the home of Commander Robert de Pass and his wife Philippa, friend of Prince Philip and lady-in-waiting to the Queen respectively. During the weekend at Petworth, West Sussex, Diana watched the Prince of Wales play polo at Cowdray Park after which there was a barbecue where Diana was seated next to the Prince. It seems that the words of comfort she spoke to him there over the death of Lord Mountbatten may have been the turning point and where the Prince – who would possibly have liked to remain a bachelor – realised that her was someone he could marry.

RIGHT Lady Diana
Spencer at the time
when rumours began of
her romance with
Prince Charles

RIGHT Lady Diana Spencer at the time when rumours began of her romance with Prince Charles

It was known nationally that the Prince thought that he had an obligation to marry and that whoever married him would be marrying into a way of life. Happiness and love were considered secondary by the Prince – a fact that was well known and documented.

However, the Prince suddenly bombarded Lady Diana with his affections which has since been recorded as bewildering the young woman. They attended a performance of Verdi's Requiem at the Royal Albert Hall with Diana's grandmother, Lady Fermoy, acting as chaperone. Not long after, Diana accompanied Prince Charles on Britannia during Cowes Week. In early September, Diana once again received an invitation from the Prince. This time it was to join him for a weekend in Balmoral for the Braemar Games. It was on this "idyllic" trip that Diana received her first taste of the media and its glare when photographers were spotted

WEDDING FEVER

across the River Dee. They tried in vain to take pictures of Diana, who successfully hid behind a tree, before walking through the woods with a headscarf concealing her identity. But, the reprieve was short-lived, and before long, the press were to know exactly who the mystery woman at Balmoral was.

Lady Diana was effectively hounded from that moment on. There were telephone calls early in the morning and the press office at Buckingham Palace

BELOW Lady Diana Spencer surrounded by press photographers shortly before the announcement of her engagement to Prince Charles

ABOVE Lady Diana Spencer leaving her home in West London. Wherever she went she was hounded by the media

declared her on her own. It was only by her sheer determination and own strength that she coped with the increasing pressure. Despite her growing love for the Prince of Wales she was doubtful about her position and the

enduring friendship with Camilla Parker Bowles. Parker Bowles, meanwhile, seemed to know everything that the couple discussed and gave Diana endless advice about how to handle the Prince and other situations and events. The press interest in Diana intensified to such an extent that even Frances Shand Kydd wrote to *The Times* demanding that the press treatment her daughter was enduring was unfair and inhumane. Diana and flatmate Carolyn began to outwit the press. Carolyn would drive off in Diana's car to foil the waiting photographers and when the coast was clear, Diana would walk in the other direction. Lady Fermoy even helped. Her own silver Golf was used in the subterfuge.

However, despite her love for the Prince she was concerned that entering a royal marriage would be difficult – even Lady Fermoy (the Queen Mother's lady-in-waiting) advised her as such. The Prince's friends were all middle-aged and completely different to Diana and then, of course, there was the ever-present Mrs Parker Bowles to consider.

On Friday 6 February 1981, the Prince of Wales asked Lady Diana Spencer to be his wife. Diana was

LEFT Journalists questioning Diana as she gets into her car, after her engagement to Prince Charles was announced

euphoric and celebrated with her flatmates that night. A few days later, the future Princess of Wales flew to Australia with her mother and stepfather to enjoy some time of seclusion and rest.

The engagement was officially announced on 24 February 1981 and from that time on Diana's life was never quite hers again. Once the engagement was official it was also time for Diana to stop calling the Prince of Wales "Sir" and she was allowed to call him Charles.

There was no-one to greet the young Diana when she arrived at Clarence House for her first night at the Queen Mother's residence. There was no advice and no formal training for the life that awaited her. Diana realised that her small wardrobe would no longer do and engaged her sister's friend, Anna Harvey, fashion editor at *Vogue* to help her build a formal wardrobe. By March, Diana was housed in Buckingham Palace where she had a second-floor

apartment and felt alone and vulnerable. Prince Charles's friendship with Camilla Parker Bowles was still strong and Diana felt that she was not the only one with a claim to the Prince.

On the other hand, Diana, her mother and a small team were busy working away within Buckingham Palace to organise the wedding that was so eagerly awaited by the Royal family, the media and the nation at large.

ABOVE Lady Diana Spencer in 1981

RIGHT Charles and Diana attend their first public engagement together, a recital at London's Goldsmith's Hall in aid of the Royal Opera House Development Appeal

LEFT Charles, with his fiancée Lady Diana Spencer outside Buckingham Palace, after announcing their engagement

Chapter 5

Marriage and the Royal Family

DIANA SPENT THE EVE OF HER wedding to Prince Charles at Clarence House where she woke early to the noise of the crowds singing along the Mall. The crowds had been gathering along the wedding processional route for days and mood among the spectators was happy and jolly. On 29 July 1981, Diana was dressed by David and Elizabeth Emanuel who had designed her wedding dress and was attended to by Barbara Daly who was responsible for her make-up and Kevin Shanley, her hairdresser. Diana was worried about the walk her father would have to make down the aisle of St Paul's Cathedral as he was recovering from a recent stroke. Despite his recent illness, the Earl managed admirably to escort his youngest daughter down the aisle in front of more than 750 million people globally. It was a happy buoyant day for the entire nation. The wedding guests enjoyed a royal wedding breakfast while the young bride dreamed of the happiness that seemingly lay ahead. The new Princess of Wales was to be disappointed.

The honeymoon took place at Broadlands in Hampshire before they joined Britannia for a cruise around the Mediterranean. But, underneath the façade of the happy couple, Diana was nursing a growing problem. The eating disorder bulimia nervosa had taken hold of her mind and her body. The problems had started during her

engagement to Prince Charles when the pressure on her was immense. The honeymoon also did little to dissuade the Princess that her husband's friendship with Camilla Parker Bowles was confined to the back burner – he wore a pair of cufflinks to dinner one evening with two "Cs" entwined. Slowly, but surely, Diana began to realise that the friendship would overshadow her own marriage.

At the end of the honeymoon the couple travelled to Balmoral where they joined the rest of the Royal family. The couple stayed on the estate between August and October where the Princess was expected to conform to life as a public figure with retained feelings and composure. But, underneath, Diana was alone and worried. Her illness was becoming worse and she was suspicious of her husband's dealings with his friend, Mrs Parker Bowles.

The Princess, herself, was set to become a phenomenon. But first, she discovered she was pregnant.

Chapter 6

Motherhood

DESPITE THE LONELINESS – DIANA did not even turn to her close friends – prolonged illness, arguments, recriminations and heartache, there was love between the royal couple. Diana was besotted with her husband, and he in turn loved her in his own way. There were moments of happiness amidst the angst and difficulties.

However, the Prince seemed unable, or unwilling to support his new wife with her troubles and their relationship was heading on a downward spiral. It is well documented that at this time the young Princess made repeated threats to end her life. Like many suffering from too much pressure, no real support and a serious illness, these threats were a cry for help rather than a real desire to succeed in carrying out the threat. The Princess, pregnant or not, was in crisis

RIGHT The Princess of Wales leaves the Guildhall in London on the day she announced she was pregnant with her first child

FAR RIGHT A pregnant Princess of Wales visits the Isles of Scilly, April 1982

and felt that her husband's continual dismay and lack of support did nothing to alleviate the situation. The bulimia nervosa was rooted firmly in the childhood she had experienced where Diana needed understanding for her feelings of guilt and loneliness, which due to social attitudes at the time was sadly overlooked. Now, as a mother-to-be and young woman in one of the highest profile positions she could possibly have taken on, she desperately needed that same understanding. It was not forthcoming from those around her and she felt desperate.

In public, as always, the Princess of Wales appeared happy and relaxed and the crowds went wild for her. No-one it seems, could get enough of the Princess of Wales. Diana had thought that once she became the wife of the heir to the throne she would somehow pale again into obscurity. Not so. The public, wherever she went, were there to see her in their droves. It completely took both Prince Charles and his new wife aback.

At this time, the Prince did everything he could to comfort his wife and gently guided her through what was a difficult time. But, he soon became indifferent at the constant tears from Diana and the pleas to back out of royal engagements.

Morning sickness proved to be a tough time for the new mother-to-be. The pregnancy was officially announced on 5 November 1981 but at the same time it was becoming apparent that the Royal family were beginning to see Charles's wife as a "problem". On the outside, however, Diana was a shining success. Newspapers were constantly full of articles about her while her face adorned magazine covers everywhere.

William Arthur Philip Louis was born on 21 June 1982. The baby caused a stir across the nation. The Princess

RIGHT The Princess of Wales looking very slender

BELOW Prince Charles with his baby son, Prince William at Kensington Palace

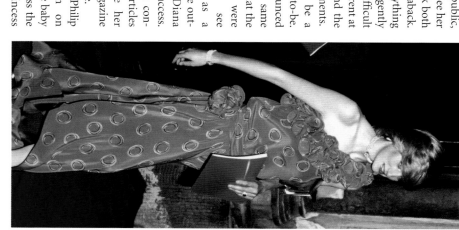

had provided the Crown with a future King and crowds greeted the Prince and Princess of Wales as they arrived back at Kensington Palace following William's birth.

Perhaps after all the disillusionment, motherhood provided the young Princess with some purpose. However, Diana was suffering from post-natal depression. By this time she was painfully thin and the tabloids were beginning to stir up rumours as to what could possibly be wrong with the Princess. One cited anorexia. The ball had started to roll and more gossip in the press and among royal circles began to materialise. The press and the nation wanted the fairytale to be as perfect as everyone believed it was – however the cracks were becoming more evident and the gossip continued. The press claims steadily became more and more outrageous and it is well known that the media gossip did indeed hurt the Princess further. Meanwhile, Diana had very little contact with her mother, Frances Shand Kydd.

The trip to Australia and New Zealand in 1983 was perhaps a turning point for the Princess. There were still tensions between the royal couple but

William accompanied his parents which made the trip easier for his mother. By now Diana was attracting worldwide attention and there were far more photographers and crowds than there would have been for any other royal couple. In fact, by the time they reached

LEFT Princess Diana and Prince Charles arrive for a state reception in New Zealand

RIGHT The crowds are out in force in New Zealand to see Princess Diana and Prince Charles

Brisbane the crowd was more than 100,000 strong. For once, the Diana that so desperately needed approval, was beginning to feel that she gained it from the crowds that so absolutely adored her. It was to mark the beginning of her

love affair with the peoples of many nations and was to remain that way to the end of her life.

However, Charles did not understand why the crowds loved his wife quite so much. He was almost in the background as people chanted her name and cheered loudly as she approached them. It was almost sad for the man who had been used to being the centre of attention to find that his wife was completely upstaging him. It was also Diana's appeal that began to hurt the couple's marriage along with the undermining that Charles's friends seemed intent on orchestrating.

Then on 14 February 1984 it was officially announced that the Prince and Princess of Wales were expecting their second baby. Henry Charles Albert David, known as Harry, was born on 15 September 1984.

Diana proved to be a successful mother; she was modern in her approach and put her children first, rearranging her life around them. Her desire was to give them as normal a life as possible while preparing them for their future roles. It seems as if the way the Princess brought up the boys from the beginning with love and support,

and the insistence that they learn about other people and their lives, has stood the two Princes in good stead in their own lives.

BELOW Princess Diana leaving St Mary's Hospital, London with her new-born son Prince Harry

Chapter 7

Charitable Work

RIGHT Princess Diana making a speech at the Centrepoint Conference for the Homeless

FAR RIGHT Princess Diana attending a ball at the Albert Hall for the Birthright charity, October 1985

THE PRINCESS'S CHARITABLE work began not long after Harry's birth when she took over as president of Barnardo's from Princess Margaret. Her rapport with the people she met while working as president was incredible and she came very much into her own. She became a champion for the rights of those who were disadvantaged and did more than any other person during the 20th century to highlight the plight of those affected by HIV or AIDS. She almost single-handedly changed the way that sufferers were portrayed globally and showed the world that it was impossible to catch HIV or AIDS by touching someone.

The Princess worked with Centrepoint, the national charity that improves the lives of young people who find themselves homeless. The

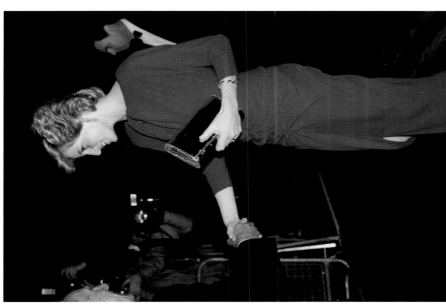

charity provides a range of accommodation including short-stay hostels, emergency night shelters as well as working with young single parents, ex-offenders and on other projects aimed at the young homeless. It also seeks to raise awareness of the plight of these young people. Today, Prince William carries on the work his mother began in his role as Patron of Centrepoint.

The National AIDS Trust was also supported by the Princess. The NAT is the UK's leading independent campaign and policy charity that aims to influence attitudes to HIV and AIDS and to change decisions that impact on the lives of those affected. The charity researches current issues and identifies solutions as well as working to educate people and campaign for change where necessary. The NAT also seeks to raise awareness through the media and by organising events and works with other HIV organisations to represent the needs of those with HIV and AIDS nationwide. World AIDS Day and the Diana, Princess of Wales, Lecture on HIV and AIDS are important events in the charity's calendar.

The Leprosy Mission was also a charity close to the Princess's heart. This leading international Christian development mission was founded in 1874 and has worked ever since to help those affected by leprosy in South Asia, Africa and the East Asia and Pacific region. The charity is run by a secretariat in London that has 28 national councils and more than 2,000 national and international field staff. The aim of the charity is to work in education, medical treatment, rehabilitation and detection of the disease which is still very much in evidence today. Those at most risk are the vulnerable poverty-stricken people who have little knowledge of the disease from which they suffer and the charity strives to help in human rights issues of those affected as well as by working towards healthier living conditions and supporting local health systems.

The Royal Marsden Hospital in West London is the leading cancer hospital that treats patients across the UK. The hospital organises a number of events and challenges each year to help with its fundraising activities. The idea of using state-of-the-art technology is to allow patients to spend as little time in the hospital as possible so that they may recuperate at home with their families. Great Ormond Street Hospital Children's Charity is the pioneering hospital dedicated to treating more

than 100,000 children each year. The charity has a substantial effect on the care and treatment provided for

RIGHT Prince Harry in the grounds of the Mants'ase children's home launching his charity 'Sentebale'

FAR RIGHT Princess Diana chats with ballerinas at the London headquarters of the English National Ballet

the world's leading ballet companies that is dedicated to taking classic ballet to audiences everywhere at affordable prices to make sure that ballet is available to all. The company remains committed to maximising accessibility and is a world leader in its education and outreach activities. The Education and Community Unit works in various communities when the company is touring to help establish relationships with diverse audiences while seeking to encourage understanding of this traditional art form.

The Concert for Diana was held on 1 July 2007 in the new Wembley Stadium to celebrate the life of the late Princess of Wales. Organised by the Princess's sons, Prince William and Prince Harry, the proceeds from the event will go to the charities chosen by the Princes including the

seriously ill children by adding to the ever-stretched NHS funds available.

The English National Ballet is one of

newly formed Sentebale which was founded by Prince Harry and Prince Seeiso from Lesotho that is designed to help the area's children and young people. The charity, which was formed in April 2006, aims to particularly help children and young people who have been orphaned as a result of AIDS. The name Sentebale means "forget me not" and was chosen by the young Princes in honour of both their mothers. Prince Harry has chosen to continue the work started by his mother, while Prince Seeiso lost his own mother, Queen Mamohato in 2003.

Following the Princess's death in 1997, the Diana, Princess of Wales Memorial Fund was established in September that year as an independent grant-giving charity to continue the humanitarian work started by the Princess. The charity works to support organisations working in the UK and overseas in areas that were close to the Princess's heart including those affected by HIV and AIDS as well as communities affected by landmines.

Chapter 8

Divorce

AFTER 10 YEARS OF LIFE AS A VERY public figure, Diana's life was about to change with the advent of divorce from Charles. There were two major things that contributed to the breakdown. The shadow that had been ever-present over the marriage was undoubtedly Camilla while the second factor was the way in which Diana upstaged and outshone her husband in their public lives through no fault of her own. Diana had glamour, and her genuine ability to communicate with all, especially those such as the elderly, sick and infirm as well as the young, gave her a modern edge that hitherto the royal family had lacked. Her popularity was like nothing ever seen

before and Charles resented her for it. The Queen was particularly appreciative of what Diana brought to the royal family and was pleased with the attention that her daughter-in-law was gaining. It gave the "firm", as the royal family are known, a new outlook and a new prestige for the monarchy that the Queen welcomed.

But the Prince and Princess of Wales drifted further and further apart and at Ascot in 1992 they left the racecourse together in a show of solidarity. However, a few miles down the road the Prince dropped the Princess by her own car and they travelled separately. On 9 December 1992, an official statement was released to break the news that Prince Charles and Diana, Princess of Wales were separating. One week prior to the announcement, Diana had been

to visit her sons at school to let them know the news. Diana remained at Kensington Palace while the Prince took refuge at Highgrove.

On 28 February 1996, Diana agreed to an uncontested divorce at Charles's request. Although Diana would retain the right to call herself the Princess of Wales, she was to lose the title of HRH... much to the public's disgust. The following four months saw negotiations take place between the two sides with a decree nisi being granted on 15 July 1996. On 28 August 1996, six weeks later, the decree absolute finally dissolved the Wales's marriage. Her estimated settlement was reported to be around £17 million.

Chapter 9

Other relationships and life after Charles

HAVING FELT TRAPPED IN HER marriage, the born-again-single Diana was soon romantically linked with a string of men before finding what seemed to be her true love. While there had been rumours and allegations of extra-marital activities with men such as James Hewitt, Diana was now free to live life to the full.

She soon became enamoured with art dealer Oliver Hoare after the two met at the Chelsea Harbour Gym. For a time it seemed as if this relationship was made to last as the pair enjoyed dining out as well as their mutual love of keep fit but Hoare called off the romance following a series of phone calls. Described by police as nuisance calls, these were

allegedly made by Diana and caused much embarrassment for the Princess after coming to public knowledge in the national press.

The next man to enter her life was England rugby star Will Carling. Again, the two shared the same gym and could often be seen over a cup of coffee but rumour had it that their relationship was far more intense. Carling got on well with Princes William and Harry – both big rugby fans – and even presented them with England rugby shirts but it was never going to work out for Diana with a married man. Although neither divulged any details of their relationship, Carling's marriage to TV presenter Julia ended in acrimony with

FAR RIGHT Diana had a strong friendship with Will Carling

his wife publicly blaming the Princess of Wales for their troubles.

Another man to gain Diana's affection was heart surgeon Dr Hasnar Khan, whom she had previously met while engaged in various charity work. Khan had the ability to relieve the pressure Diana felt by the intrusive media but in the end didn't want to cope with life in the public eye himself. Despite numerous romantic meetings – including spending time on his yacht on the south coast – Khan ended his relationship with Diana.

There are rumours that the Princess of Wales enjoyed a romantic liaison with Canadian rock star Bryan Adams but these have never been confirmed or denied. While it is not in doubt that they met in 1996, the extent of their relationship has never been divulged. Adams's ex-girlfriend has claimed there was more than anyone ever let on while Paul Burrell mentions an unnamed rock star in his book *A Royal Duty*. Whatever the truth, it was with Dodi Al Fayed that Diana, Princess of Wales, appeared to find true happiness.

With Prince Charles declaring his

RIGHT Diana was very fond of Dodi al Fayed

intention to host a 50th birthday party for Camilla Parker-Bowles at his Highgrove home, Diana felt the need to get out of the country. She accepted an open invitation from Harrods owner Mohammed Al Fayed and took William and Harry to St Tropez for a holiday in the sun. Dodi joined the holiday part way through and even rented a disco so that Diana and the boys could dance without press intrusion.

Once the Princes had returned to Balmoral for their holiday with their father and Diana had flown to Milan for the funeral of Gianni Versace, she once again sought the company of Dodi. It has been suggested that Charles's willingness to be more open about his relationship with Camilla led

RIGHT Diana attends the Requiem Mass for Gianni Versace shortly before her own premature death

Diana in turn to be less worried about public reaction to the men in her life.

Her holiday was interrupted by a trip to Bosnia fulfilling a charitable engagement regarding landmines, but she soon returned to the Sardinian coast where the pair were captured on camera having fun on a jet-ski. It seemed that, for perhaps the first time in her life, Diana had found her true soul mate and was enjoying just being herself without having to worry about what anyone else thought. Indeed, she is reported to have told her friend Lady Elsa Bowker that she adored Dodi, adding "I have never been so happy."

Diana and Dodi's body language indicated the depth of feelings they had for each other and this seemed to be confirmed when they visited a jewellers in Monte Carlo. She was extremely interested in a £130,000 diamond ring but it has never been proven whether this was an engagement ring or merely a token of Dodi's affection. What nobody could have foreseen, though, was the terrible tragedy that was to strike a few days later.

Chapter 10

Paris and One Fateful Night

DIANA AND DODI HAD SPENT THE summer trying to enjoy their holiday despite the paparazzi constantly invading their privacy. There had been grainy pictures – taken at great distance with a telephoto lens – published in the tabloids of the pair relaxing on the Al Fayed yacht in the Mediterranean. With the photographer who captured them on film kissing reportedly being paid $3 million, it was little wonder that there was such a frenzy for pictures.

The couple flew from Sardinia to Paris on 30 August with Diana intending to return to Kensington Palace the following day. They dined that evening in the Imperial Suite at the Ritz, owned by Dodi's father, but were tiring of the

waiting hordes of cameramen. In an attempt to divert their attention, Dodi's car was driven back to his apartment near the Arc de Triomphe by his chauffeur as a decoy but this ruse did not fool the press who were patiently waiting outside, ready to give chase in cars and on motorbikes.

The Ritz's deputy chief of security, Henri Paul, was enlisted to drive the Princess and Dodi and the group emerged from the rear entrance of the hotel around midnight (Central European Time). The black bulletproof Mercedes 280SL they chose for their fateful journey was a three-year-old rental car that had a chequered history. It had previously been stolen and

PARIS AND ONE FATEFUL NIGHT

stripped for parts before being repaired by Mercedes but was hardly the best choice of vehicle for evading any pursuers as it was a heavy car that was best suited to motorway cruising and not weaving in and out of traffic in a busy city.

Diana and Dodi climbed into the car and Paul pulled away from the Ritz with the paparazzi in pursuit. All three neglected to put on their seatbelts; it would turn out to be a fatal mistake. The car drove along Rue Cambon and accelerated in an attempt to outrun the

BELOW Dodi Al Fayed, Prince Harry and Diana seen in St Tropez in the summer of 1997

ABOVE Security video of the Ritz in Paris showing Dodi Al Fayed

cars and bikes that were tailing them. By the time it entered the underpass below Pont de l'Alma, the Mercedes was travelling at an estimated 90–120mph in an area where there is a 30mph speed limit.

The 660' tunnel was well lit but the approach does not lend itself to high-speed driving as it veers right, then left

PARIS AND ONE FATEFUL NIGHT

before there is a dip in the road. The driver lost control of the vehicle as it entered the tunnel and the car ricocheted off the wall and smashed into the pillars supporting the roof. It rolled and came to a halt against the 13th pillar, facing the direction in which it had just come from. Although fitted with anti-lock brakes, the car left a 53' skid mark according to the police, which is a clear sign that the vehicle was travelling at excessive speed.

The following paparazzi, while shocked at the events they had just wit-

RIGHT Messages above the entrance to the tunnel where Princess Diana and Dodi Al Fayed died

nessed, began taking photos of the mangled wreckage instead of helping the stricken occupants but, these taste-less shots were later confiscated by police. The driver of the car died instantly and the force of the crash was so brutal that parts of the radiator were allegedly found embedded in Henri Paul's body as it was slumped over the steering wheel. Dodi Al Fayed was also killed instantly in the collision but

Princess Diana was clinging to life when help arrived at approximately 12.40am. (A photograph of the injured Princess having an oxygen mask placed on her face was published by the Italian Chi magazine in 2006 to much derision.)

Emergency medical personnel fought to keep her alive and desperately tried to treat her severe head and chest injuries while firemen sought to extricate her from the wreckage. Unfortunately, cutting through the roof was hampered by the reinforced steel used in the construction of the car and the procedure took around an hour and a half instead of the minutes it would have taken the highly trained experts to gain access to a standard vehicle. The Princess, still bleeding profusely internally in her chest, was finally removed from the car and taken to La Pitié-Salpêtrière hospital.

There have been many different versions of the injuries Diana suffered and how and where she was treated but the undeniable fact is that doctors en route to and at the hospital continued their fight to save her

ABOVE A cameraman films the point of the fatal car accident in Paris

life. Her left pulmonary vein was ruptured, however, and Diana went into cardiac arrest. They tried to revive her first by external chest massage and then by direct massage to her heart but it all proved to be in vain. Her injuries were too great for her to survive and it was at 4.00am CET on 31 August 1997 that Diana, Princess of Wales, was pronounced dead. The only person to have survived the crash was bodyguard

Trevor Rees-Jones, who suffered concussion and bruising but had no recollection of the accident whatsoever. He had been the only occupant of the car wearing a seat-belt.

With the Royal family holidaying in Scotland at Balmoral, Prince Charles broke the news of Diana's death to their sons, Princes William and Harry, while an official announcement from Buckingham Palace declared the Queen and her son to be "deeply shocked and distressed" by the events in Paris.

In the aftermath of the tragedy, it was reported that Henri Paul had consumed a large amount of alcohol – the equivalent of 10 glasses of wine – before the accident and there were also drugs in his bloodstream (the anti-depressant Prozac and Tiapride, a drug used to combat alcoholism). His family vehemently denied that he had been drunk when he got behind the wheel and security camera footage later released seemed to back up their claims. This provided more ammunition for those who are convinced that there was a conspiracy to prevent Diana and Dodi from marrying but more of this in a later chapter.

Although the French authorities arrested nine of the photographers who had been chasing the car and charged them with involuntary manslaughter, these charges were later dropped when a formal investigation laid the blame for the accident solely on Henri Paul. There were also claims that the Mercedes had hit a white Fiat Uno in the tunnel but this has never been substantiated and so the debate – and investigation – continues.

Chapter 11

A Country in Mourning

NO-ONE COULD HAVE IMAGINED the scale of the grief felt by the British public once they awoke in disbelief on the morning of Sunday 31 August 1997 to the news that Princess Diana had died. Devastated by the events in Paris, millions of people were drawn to London to share in their mourning, many of them leaving bouquets of flowers at the gates of the Princess's home at Kensington Palace. Within a few days, the whole area was a sea of colour that the news cameras broadcast around the world.

Such was the extent of the public's grief that many patiently queued for 12 hours or more to sign one of the numerous books of condolences that had been hurriedly opened around the capital. More than 3,500 telephone lines were set up to deal with the volume of callers who wished to donate money to the Memorial Fund set up in Diana's memory and this fund soon accumulated almost £70 million.

It was boosted by the sales of Elton John's tribute single "Candle In The Wind 1997" which went on to sell more than 33 million copies worldwide. The song had originally been penned in 1973 in memory of actress Marilyn Monroe but the lyrics were rewritten and now included the immortal first line "Goodbye, England's Rose". Princess Diana and Elton had attended the funeral of their friend

FAR RIGHT Floral tributes and balloons spread out as far as the eye can see in the gardens of Kensington Palace

Gianni Versace just weeks before and the singer was devastated at losing another friend so soon after. He initially declined to attend Diana's funeral but relented and performed the song live in Westminster Abbey.

The royal family angered a large section of the British public by refusing to cut short their stay at Balmoral to return to London. At their Sunday service, Diana's name was not even mentioned due to the fact that it had been decided not to include her in prayers for the royal family once she had lost her HRH title. Many also felt that there should have been a Union Jack flying above Buckingham Palace at half-mast out of respect for Diana, a mood *The Express* newspaper captured perfectly with the headline "Show Us You Care". Eventually, public opinion swayed the monarchy and they returned to London with the Queen addressing the nation from the Palace on the eve of the funeral.

Princes Charles, William and Harry had previously inspected the floral tribute that had grown outside Kensington Palace, reading some of the cards, and the Duke of York and Prince Edward signed one of the books of condolences at St James' Palace. The Queen and Prince Philip were also obviously shaken by the strength of the public's feelings as they stopped their car outside Buckingham Palace to read some of the tributes to their former daughter-in-law and talk to members of the crowd.

There was no precedent for dealing with this type of situation. There was much debate about whether Diana – as the mother of the future King – should be treated as a member of the royal family or whether it should be left to the Spencer family to decide on the funeral arrangements. In the end, a semi-state funeral was decided upon and the Princess's body was flown back to Britain, accompanied by Prince Charles and Diana's sisters, Lady Jane Fellowes and Lady Sarah McCorquodale. On the journey from RAF Northolt to London, the roads were lined with thousands of people who wanted to pay their last respects to the woman Prime Minister Tony Blair had dubbed the "People's Princess".

Earl Spencer was informed of the tragedy at his South African home and he issued a statement blaming the media for her death saying that he always believed they would kill his sister in the end. He accused the editor of each publication that had paid for the highly prized photographs of Diana of having blood on their hands.

Diana's coffin was placed in St James' Palace's Chapel Royal and then moved to Kensington Palace the day before the

FAR LEFT
Prince Charles sits between his two sons, Prince William (R) and Prince Harry (L), as they leave Crathie church after hearing of the death of Diana

RIGHT (L to R)
Earl Spencer, and
Princes Harry,
William, and Charles
at the funeral in
Westminster Abbey

funeral. The streets were lined with people who were either holding a candle in silence or weeping and throwing flowers onto the hearse that contained her coffin covered in a Royal Standard. The hearse was closely followed by a limousine bearing Princes Charles, William and Harry while two cars

carrying members of Diana's family and the clergy made up the procession. Princess Diana's funeral route originally mirrored the one that had been planned for the Queen Mother but was extended due to the number of people expected to be lining the streets.

Thousands camped rough overnight

to gain a prime spot to watch the spectacle that was intended to be as near to a state funeral as possible but without the pomp and ceremony. The ceremonial funeral route soon filled up with millions of mourners that caused many to comment that such scenes had not been seen in London since the state funeral of former Prime Minister Sir Winston Churchill in 1965.

At 9.08am on Saturday 6 September, Princess Diana's coffin – adorned with three wreaths, from her sons and her brother – left Kensington Palace on a horse-drawn gun carriage and began its long journey to Westminster Abbey where the tenor bell was tolling at one-minute intervals. A wave of applause followed the cortège as it made its way down Kensington Road, to Hyde Park Corner and on to Buckingham Palace where the Union Jack was flying at half-mast for the first time in history.

The Queen – who bowed her head as Diana's coffin passed by – and other members of the royal family had come to stand at the gates as a mark of respect before the cortège continued down the Mall where it was joined at St James' Palace by Princes Philip, Charles, William and Harry as

well as Earl Spencer. The three men walked behind the coffin as well wishers called out shouts of "God bless you!" to the two boys.

The cortège arrived at Westminster Abbey where 2,000 people had been

LEFT The Union Jack flies at half-mast over Buckingham Palace

invited to make up the congregation (those whom the Abbey was unable to accommodate could watch on giant screens erected in Hyde Park). These 500 people representing some of the charities that Diana had supported. Mohamed Al Fayed and his wife were also in attendance, sharing their grief at the loss of their son and – if claims were true – their future daughter-in-law.

The service – which was watched by an estimated two billion people worldwide – began with the National Anthem as the cortège entered the Abbey before the Dean of Westminster, the Very Reverend Dr Wesley Carr, said The Bidding. The service also included readings by Diana's sisters and the Prime Minister before Elton John performed "Candle In The Wind 1997".

But it was the tribute by Earl Spencer that brought the biggest reaction both inside and outside the Abbey. He described his sister as "the very essence of compassion, of duty, of style, of beauty... who proved in the last year that she needed no royal title to continue to generate her particular brand of magic." He went on to state that she "talked endlessly of getting away from

A COUNTRY IN MOURNING

England, mainly because of the treatment she received at the hands of the newspapers" pointing out that "of all the ironies about Diana, perhaps the greatest is this; that a girl given the name of the ancient goddess of hunting was, in the end, the most hunted person of the modern age."

In what was perceived as a dig at the monarchy, Earl Spencer went on to promise to take care of Princes William

and Harry, pledging that "we, your blood family, will do all we can to continue the imaginative and loving way in which you were steering these two exceptional young men, so that their souls are not simply immersed by duty and tradition but can sing openly as you planned."

As he battled to control his emotions in order to finish his eulogy, there was an air of silence throughout the

FAR LEFT A bearer party of Welsh Guards carry the coffin of Diana into Westminster Abbey followed by (L to R) Prince Charles, Prince Harry, Earl Spencer, Prince William and the Duke of Edinburgh

LEFT The hearse carrying the coffin of Diana takes her on her final journey to the Althorp family home

RIGHT Diana is buried on a small island in the middle of the Oval Lake on the Althorp Estate

capital that was soon replaced by thunderous applause which began with those listening in the streets and that soon washed into the Abbey itself. Further hymns and prayers followed before a national one-minute's silence was observed prior to the cortège departing from the Abbey.

Following the service, the world witnessed scenes that it will probably never see again. As the hearse left Westminster Abbey, the streets were lined with people who attempted to throw flowers onto its bonnet and roof. Even bridges on the motorway were used as vantage points for people desperate to pay their last respects to the Princess of Wales.

Diana was eventually laid to rest on an island in the middle of an ornamental lake in the family grounds of Althorp. It was a private ceremony away from the reach of the press and public with the only non-family member being butler Paul Burrell. It had been decided that this was a more fitting burial site for the Princess than the nearby cemetery at Great Brington as it was feared that the small village would become a shrine.

Chapter 12

The Conspiracy Theory

LIKE MANY FAMOUS CELEBRITIES in history who have died suddenly, there are always some people who are unwilling to accept the events on face value. Take Elvis Presley, for instance, who some people believed faked his own death in August 1977 to avoid the glare of the media. Not a single year goes by without somebody claiming they have seen the King of Rock'n'Roll alive and well. There are also conspiracy theories surrounding the demise of people such as President John F Kennedy, assassinated in November 1963, and actress Marilyn Monroe who is alleged to have overdosed on sleeping pills in August 1962.

There have been numerous outspoken theories behind the crash that claimed Diana's life, many of them pointing the finger of blame at the monarchy. Of course, some people simply refuse to believe the official version of events due to the fact that none of the bodies were ever seen because of the closed caskets. Indeed, polls have shown that as much as 25% of the British public believe that the Princess of Wales was murdered. Here we take a look at a few of the most common beliefs...

One view is that the monarchy ordered Diana to be killed because she was becoming a threat to the throne. It is true that she was without doubt the person who held most affection in the hearts of the public but there are few who can realistically believe that the due to the fact that Prince Charles's popularity was sinking lower and lower to previously unthinkable levels. There have been claims that MI6 agents secretly bugged Diana throughout her life as a royal and it has been suggested that they were the ones who leaked the Squidgygate tapes in order to discredit the Princess of Wales. Indeed, it emerged in December 2006 that the US secret service was listening in on Diana's telephone conversations in the hours leading up to her death. This has been confirmed by the Americans but was carried out without the knowledge of MI6.

LEFT Martine Monteil, head of the Paris judiciary police, speaks to the press on the site of the 1997 car crash

Queen or Prince Philip authorised an assassination. There is another line of thought that rogue MI6 agents acted on their own initiative because they could foresee the end of the British monarchy

One belief is that Diana faked her own death to escape the media but this has been universally ridiculed because no-one can accept that a caring mother such as the Princess of Wales would go

RIGHT An inquest into the deaths of Diana and Dodi Al Fayed at the Royal Courts of Justice, took place almost ten years after the pair died

to such lengths that would include not being able to see her beloved sons grow up. The people who claim this theory to be true argue that the crash could have been an attempt to fake her own death that went disastrously wrong and cite Diana's admission to a reporter just six hours before her death that she was

going to withdraw from public life as proof of this.

The version often touted by Dodi's father, Mohammed Al Fayed, however, is that Henri Paul's blood samples were switched in an effort to portray him as a drunk while covering up the establishment's plan to prevent Diana from

THE CONSPIRACY THEORY

marrying a Muslim. There have been numerous claims about the depth of feelings the two had for each other, ranging from Diana accepting Dodi's marriage proposal on that fateful night to Diana being pregnant with Dodi's baby. No-one has ever been able to present concrete evidence about any of these theories and the debate rages on today.

Mohammed Al Fayed has campaigned for the truth to be made public ever since that night and has made several attempts to bring this about. In November 1999 he lost a legal battle to be allowed to participate in the inquest but in December 2006 won the right for the preliminary hearings ahead of the full official inquest to be held in public. Three months later, the Harrods tycoon won another verdict when three High Court judges ruled that the inquest should be held in front of a jury and not just the deputy royal coroner Baroness Butler-Sloss. The Baroness stepped down from her role in April 2007 citing she did not have sufficient experience to oversee an inquest with a jury, and Lord Justice Scott Baker took

over the reins in June. There was further debate over whether the jury should be made up of members of the royal household – because Diana had been a member of the royal family – or the public.

Whatever the outcome of these arguments, the inquest is due to begin in October 2007 and is expected to last somewhere between four to eight months. Whether the eventual decision will appease those who believe there was a conspiracy remains to be seen…

Chapter 13

A Life Remembered and Diana's Legacy

THE IMMEDIATE AFTERMATH OF Diana's death brought about a "war" between the Spencers and the Windsors. Diana's sisters were appointed executors of her Will that obviously saw Princes William and Harry named as the two major beneficiaries. There were claims by Diana's butler Paul Burrell, however, that the family were so intent on destroying links with the royal family that they even went as far as shredding some of the Princess's personal correspondence.

Burrell was invited to join the Diana, Princess of Wales Memorial Committee whose aim was to advise the government on how best the Princess should be remembered. Such is the fondness and high regard felt for Diana by the

public at large, there have been many memorials erected in her memory. Mohammed Al Fayed erected a memorial to Dodi and Diana at Harrods on 12 April 1998, and unveiled a second, grander memorial in September 2005.

Two of the main memorials erected in London in honour of Diana have been a playground and a fountain. The Diana, Princess of Wales Memorial Playground was built near her home in Kensington Gardens and was opened by her goddaughter Domenica Monckton. The centerpiece of the playground boasts a huge wooden pirate ship for children to play on while other attractions include teepees, a sensory trail and other structures.

Charles's lawyers MPs demand inquiry
HER TEA
The Queen weeps for REAL heroes (and perhaps over the new scandal engulfing her family)
Be careful Paul, nobody has ever been closer to a member of my family than you were to Diana. There
Jakob Dylan • Ruth Rendell • Matthew Parris • Alan Partridge
FREE 28 PAGE MAGAZINE INSIDE
Gordon Ramsay cooks Christmas
Save 40% on cookery books
THE TIMES
SATURDAY NOVEMBER 9 2002
A moment of peace for Prince facing turmoil a
DAILY EXPRESS
The World's Greatest Newspaper
Burrell and Barrymore
Express reveals the amazing friendship between shamed TV star and Diana's butler
ONLY 20P TODAY
QUEEN BREAKS DOWN IN TEARS
WORLD Exclusive
DAILY Mirror
NEWSPAPER OF THE YEAR
45p
THE TRUTH
All too much
HOW BARR COMFORTE
WORTH £25 EVERY READER
DAILY EXPRESS
TODAY ONLY 35p
FREE Sparklers for every reader for bonfire night
GET THEM AT ASDA TODAY
Biggest sensation in legal his is cleared and says: 'Thank yo

The committee set up to oversee the construction of the Princess Diana Memorial Fountain in Hyde Park began by choosing a design from the 10,000 that were submitted. The winning designer was US architect Kathryn Gustafson who planned a Cornish granite stone ring to sit on the site like a necklace. Water is introduced at the highest point and travels both east – flowing over steps – and west where it resembles a babbling brook before meeting in the reflection pool before being pumped up to start the cycle again. There have been notable critics of this memorial, particularly the Princess's late mother Frances Shand Kydd who accused the design of lacking in grandeur.

The Queen opened the Fountain in July 2004 at a ceremony attended by Prince Charles, Earl Spencer and Princes William and Harry – the first time since Diana's

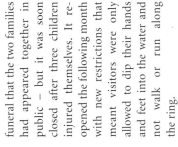

funeral that the two families had appeared together in public – but it was soon closed after three children injured themselves. It re-opened the following month with new restrictions that meant visitors were only allowed to dip their hands and feet into the water and not walk or run along the ring.

The Diana, Princess of Wales, Memorial Walk winds its way in a figure of eight through four of the capital's royal parks. Measuring approximately seven miles long, the Walk encompasses three of the palaces (Kensington, Buckingham and St James') and two man-sions (Spencer House and Clarence House) associated with the Princess.

Perhaps the most emotive memorial for Diana is the museum at her family home. Set within the grounds where she is buried, Althorp boasts an exhibition of

photographs, old toys, clothing and school reports that only a family can put together. There is a place of honour for her wedding dress and also a room devoted to the tributes that were paid after her death. Thousands of people make a pilgrimage to this place every year but for those who are unable to visit Althorp, some of the exhibits are shown off around the world and were well received in America in 2005.

As previously mentioned, the Diana, Princess of Wales, Memorial Fund was set up to manage the public donations and the income from the sales of Elton John's single, and Paul Burrell was enlisted to help with the administration of this as well. Burrell would find himself charged with stealing 310 of the Princess's personal items but the case collapsed and he was exonerated in 2002.

The Fund itself has not been a stranger to controversy during its short existence; it has handed out £13.5 million to American charities including sponsorship for Israeli students in the US and announced plans costing £10 million to "raise awareness and highlight the needs and issues of young refugees and asylum seekers". Defenders of Diana's legacy argue that neither of

these causes were supported by the Princess during her life and claim that the money should be spent helping the charities that were close to her heart such as AIDs and landmine victims. The Fund was also accused of wasting more than £4 million pursuing an unsuccessful legal action against the Franklin Mint whom they insisted were cashing in illegally on the Princess's memory. The Franklin Mint counter-sued but the case was settled out of court in late 2004.

Although a memorial concert was held for Diana in the grounds of Althorp in June 1998, plans were announced in late 2006 for a Concert For Diana to be held in Wembley Stadium on 1 July 2007, the day she would have celebrated her 46th birthday. Princes William and Harry invited both sides of their family to attend with performers such as Sir Cliff Richard, Sir Elton John and Bryan Ferry chosen from their mother's favourite acts. The inclusion of songs from Andrew Lloyd Webber's West End musicals reflected the Princess's love of a wide spectrum of entertainment.

The royals came under fire in 2007 when it was announced that the

A LIFE REMEMBERED

10th anniversary memorial service would be held in the Guards' Chapel at Wellington Barracks, a venue that can only accommodate 500 people. The thousands of people who would have wanted to attend had to be content with a live television broadcast of the service by the BBC.

As with the old saying that "it's impossible to please all of the people all of the time", there will always be someone who disagrees with how Diana's memory should be honoured or cherished. Perhaps it is time to put all the bickering to one side and just remember Diana, Princess of Wales, for the inspirational woman she was.

FAR LEFT Wembley Stadium, where the Concert For Diana took place

BELOW Take That on stage, 2007

THE LITTLE BOOK OF DIANA | **91**

RIGHT An aerial view of The Princess Diana Memorial Fountain in Hyde Park

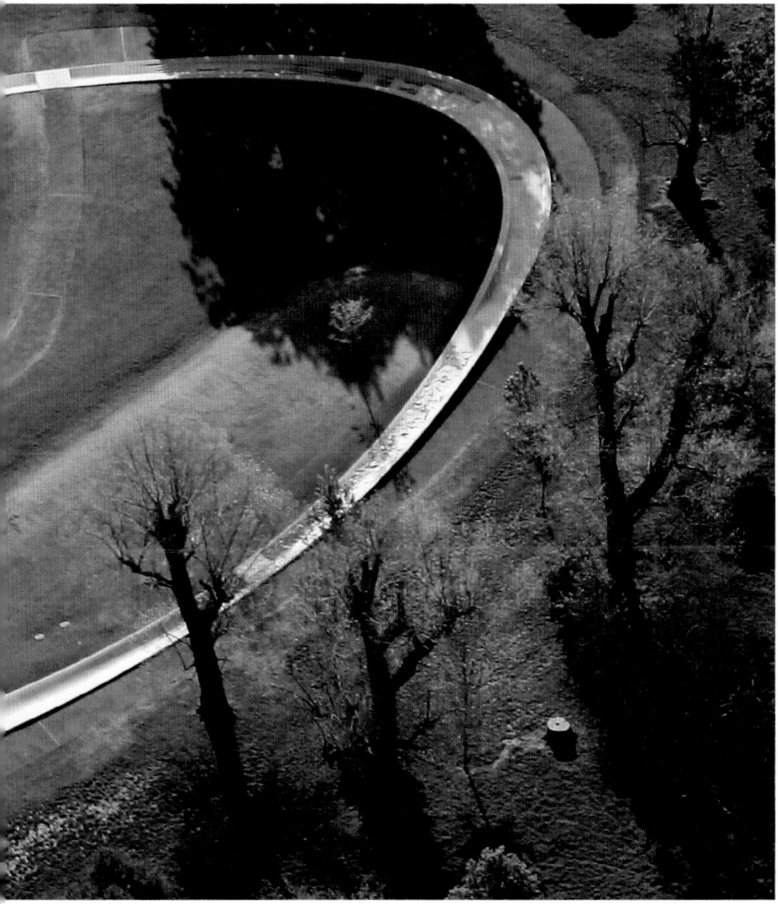

The pictures in this book were provided courtesy of

GETTY IMAGES
www.gettyimages.com

Design and artwork by Jane Stephens

Image research by Ellie Charleston

Creative Director: Kevin Gardner

Published by Green Umbrella Publishing

Publishers: Jules Gammond, Vanessa Gardner

Written by Ian and Claire Welch